GREAT PEOPLE
WHO REACHED FOR THE
STARS

Published in the UK by Scholastic Children's Books, 2021
Euston House, 24 Eversholt Street, London, NW1 1DB, UK
A division of Scholastic Limited

London ~ New York ~ Toronto ~ Sydney ~ Auckland
Mexico City ~ New Delhi ~ Hong Kong

SCHOLASTIC and associated logos are trademarks and/or
registered trademarks of Scholastic Inc.

Text © Louise Page, 2021
Illustrations © Kat Williams, 2021

ISBN 978 0702 30279 4

A CIP catalogue record for this book is available from the British Library.

Any website addresses listed in the book are correct at the time of going to print. However, please
be aware that online content is subject to change and websites can contain or offer content that is
unsuitable for children. We advise all children be supervised when using the internet.

Printed in China

Papers used by Scholastic Children's Books are made from wood grown in sustainable forests.

2 4 6 8 10 9 7 5 3 1

www.scholastic.co.uk

Louise Page

GREAT PEOPLE

WHO REACHED FOR THE

STARS

Illustrated by
Kat Williams

SCHOLASTIC

CONTENTS

- -

A GUIDE TO THE LANGUAGE USED IN THIS BOOK

- -

Experiences are the building blocks of human beings. Each of us is made up of hundreds of thousands, probably even millions, of these building blocks – these experiences. For the people in this book – and for me – some of our building blocks are experiences linked to disability, long-term illness, or similar challenges. A huge part of these experiences are the barriers that exist in society that disable us. This book aims to bring together this network of experiences, from a wide range of different people; showing that we have some shared building blocks, and some experiences that are entirely individual.

I have used language in this book that focuses in on experiences as the building blocks that make up a person. For example, I may say that someone "experiences Bipolar Disorder"; or refer to "people experiencing disability". My choice to use this language is shaped by events in my life as well as how I currently see the world.

I have made some exceptions to this use of language; specifically for Deaf, Blind and Autistic people. This is because their communities overwhelmingly prefer this language.

In this book, you will find the use of both 'Deaf' (to refer to people experiencing deafness their entire lives, and have a strong connection to the Deaf community) and 'deaf' (to refer to those experiencing deafness later in life). Again, however, it does depend on the individual's own preferences as to whether they would prefer 'Deaf' or 'deaf', or something else entirely.

I realize that not everyone will prefer the language I use. Other people experiencing disability will prefer different terminology. That's how it should be. People experiencing disability, long-term illness, or similar challenges are a large and complicated body of people, and the language we use to describe ourselves should be as wide and varied as the lives we live.

Through reading this book I hope that you will enjoy hearing about the experiences of people from all walks of life, from all over the world, from ancient times until the present day.

Louise Page

- -

TIMELINE

750 BCE: Homer lives

1770: Ludwig van Beethoven is born

1880: Helen Keller is born

1822: Harriet Tubman is born

1827: Ludwig van Beethoven dies

1907: Frida Kahlo is born

1913: Harriet Tubman dies

1918: Abraham Nemeth is born

1929: Yayoi Kusama is born

1942: Stephen Hawking is born

1943: Judith Scott is born

1946: Kay Redfield Jamison is born

1947: David Blunkett is born

1954: Frida Kahlo dies

1955: Zhang Haidi is born

1956: Elyn Saks is born

1957: Fatima Al-Aqel is born

1965: Sudha Chandran is born

1965: Evelyn Glennie is born

1967: Jean Christophe Parisot is born

1968: Helen Keller dies

1970s: Social Model of Disability
developed by people experiencing disability

1972: Lisa Bufano is born

1972: Liz Carr is born

1977: **Emmanuel Ofosu Yeboah** is born

1980: **Jess Thom** is born

~~ound~~ 1981: **Ola Abu Al Ghaib** is born

1985: **Adam Pearson** is born

1994: **Winnie Harlow** is born

1994: **Ellie Simmonds** is born

2003: **Greta Thunberg** is born

2005: **Judith Scott** dies

2006: **UN Convention on the Human Rights of Disabled Persons**

2012: **Fatima Al-Aqel** dies

2013: **Lisa Bufano** dies

2013: **Abraham Nemeth** dies

2013: *Under the Skin* is released

2018: **Stephen Hawking** dies

"REMEMBER TO LOOK UP AT THE STARS AND NOT DOWN AT YOUR FEET."

Stephen Hawking
(1942–2018)

For his seventh birthday, Stephen got a clockwork model train set, but it didn't work properly. For months now he has been dreaming of a new train set that runs on electricity. He is pretty sure that an electric train would work better than his clockwork one.

Today, Stephen's parents are both on holiday. That's why he's going to the bank on his own. He's going to withdraw all of his savings and finally buy that electric train set.

When he gets home, his hands tremble as he opens the packaging, lays out the train tracks, and sets the train running. He holds his breath as he watches the train make its first loop of the track … only this train doesn't work the way he had imagined either. It goes unevenly fast, and then slow. It looks nothing like the movement of a real train. It is extremely annoying. If only he understood how the train worked, then maybe he could fix it. If only he could find some way to have control over the electric mechanism, so that it would work like it did in his imagination. At first he doesn't know what to do with his frustration but then he has an idea. It is in this moment that Stephen decides that when he grows up, he will learn to understand how everything works. Not just train sets, but the whole universe.

Stephen's want to understand how the world works led him to study at two of the top universities in the UK. However, at the age of twenty-one, he was struggling to put his

many scientific ideas into working order, and his teachers were getting frustrated with him.

At the same time as struggling with his studies, Stephen began to have unexplained accidents and falls. Eventually his parents sent him to see a doctor. He was diagnosed with Motor Neurone Disease. This was terrifying for Stephen. He was told that he didn't have long to live. However, he used the energy that built up behind his experiences to focus doubly hard on his work. From that day onwards, he made many discoveries in the field of **physics**.

Despite what the doctors told Stephen, he went on to live a long life. He used his time on Earth to fulfil the promise he showed as a child, watching his toy train circle the tracks, and wondering how it worked. As an adult, he learnt how many things worked – including making discoveries about **black holes**. He wrote a number of important books to help people understand the way the universe functions. He died in 2018 at the age of 76.

- - - - - - - - - - - - - - - - -

EXPLORE MORE:
Stephen used his imagination to solve scientific problems. If you could solve any problem with your imagination, what would it be?

- - - - - - - - - - - - - - - - -

WORDS TO KNOW
Black holes: created when a star collapses in on itself. They are called "black" holes because even light cannot escape from them due to their gravity being so strong.
Physics: a type of science that looks at nature, space, time and matter. Most physicists are also very good at maths.

Stephen Hawking experienced **Motor Neurone Disease**. This means that his brain, and the branch-like system attached to his brain, stopped working properly, leading to his muscles being unable to move as they did before he developed the condition.

"KEEP YOUR FACE TO THE SUNSHINE AND YOU CANNOT SEE THE SHADOWS."

Helen Keller

(1880–1968)

We join Helen Keller one summer morning in Alabama, a state in the USA. She is angry. Her teacher, Anne, is trying to help her understand the word "water". Helen has to work extra hard to understand her teacher's lessons, because she can't see or hear anything. It's been that way since she was ill as a toddler.

Anne pours water over Helen's hand, and then uses her fingers to spell w-a-t-e-r on Helen's skin. Helen relies completely on her sense of touch to understand the world, so the word for "water" is a difficult one to understand. She gets more and more frustrated as Anne repeats the lesson over and over, until she feels like she is about to explode. Full of anger, she throws her toy doll on to the floor, smashing it into pieces.

Anne is very patient, she doesn't

WATER

tell Helen off. Instead, Anne puts a hat on Helen's head, signalling that they are going on a trip outside. This makes Helen very excited – she loves going outside! Sometimes, when she feels trapped, and like no one will ever understand her, Helen goes outside and lies on the grass. She likes feeling the coolness of the plants in the garden against her skin.

Once being outside with nature has calmed Helen down, Anne takes her over to a water pump. She puts Helen's hand into the stream of water flowing out of the pump, and once again spells w-a-t-e-r on to her skin. This time, something about the magic of being outside helps Helen to understand. She learns the word "water". Helen learnt many words

that day, and Anne was her teacher and companion for the rest of her life.

As she got older, Helen's hunger to learn only grew. Some people who are Deaf can communicate using **sign language**. However, as Helen was also Blind she couldn't communicate in this way, as she was unable to see the signs. Instead, Anne continued to translate what other people were saying to Helen via finger spelling. Helen could read books by using **braille**. She learnt to speak by using her hands to trace people's mouth movements, and then copying them. When Helen was still a teenager, she took up studies at **Harvard University**. She was the first person who was both Deaf and Blind to get a degree at Harvard. She used the skills she learnt from Anne, and from university, to campaign for disabled people's rights. Helen was also a **feminist**, standing up for women's rights to education, and a **socialist** who stood up for worker's rights. Helen wrote many books and articles on these issues, including an autobiography called *The Story of My Life*.

Helen could recognize a person from the vibration that the sound of their footsteps made. To do this, she used her body to sense sound, in a similar way to Evelyn Glennie the percussionist, who we will meet later on in this book.

EXPLORE MORE:

Throughout her life, Helen worked together with other people to achieve amazing things. This didn't just include her work with Anne, but also the groups she gathered when giving feminist speeches and talks about disability and socialism. Helen inspired people to work together using her words. If you were going to give a speech, what would it be about?

WORDS TO KNOW

Braille: a form of writing which uses raised bumps to shape letters and words. This allows people who are Blind to read through touch.

Feminist: a feminist is someone who believes that there should be equal rights between all genders.

Harvard University: one of the top universities in the USA.

Sign Language: a language which uses signs made by the hands and facial expressions rather than spoken words. There are around 135 different sign languages around the world. Even though both countries speak English, the UK and the USA have different sign languages.

Socialist: a socialist is someone who believes that workers should own the things that they make, and the ways of producing those things. This means that they get fair pay for their work.

Helen Keller was born both **Deaf and Blind**. This means that she couldn't see or hear. However, she learnt to speak by feeling other people's faces and mimicking the shapes their mouths made whilst they spoke.

LIFE DOESN'T COME WITH READY-MADE LABELS

- -

Experiencing disability often involves being labelled. Whether that is receiving a diagnosis (the name given by the medical profession to a set of experiences) from a doctor, or being called a cruel name in an incident of bullying or a hate crime.

Labels can be useful in some circumstances, and can be important to some people's sense of identity; but they can also be upsetting or considered restrictive. It should be up to each individual person whether they use labels or not. It is important to remember that nature, and human life in particular, didn't come into existence with ready-made labels attached. All labels – including diagnoses – were invented by human beings in an attempt to make sense out of patterns they found in nature.

Labels are also not fixed things. For example, the name for a diagnosis changes over time. As a result, a modern diagnosis might have been called something completely different a few decades ago. For example, Kay Redfield Jamison's diagnosis of "Bipolar Disorder" used to be called "Manic-Depression".

The current medical system runs on diagnoses, so it can sometimes be useful to have one as shorthand for your wider experiences. Some people also find having a diagnosis a freeing experience – it may put a name to something they have experienced for a long time; and can help them to connect with other people who have the same diagnosis. However, some people experiencing disability find that having a diagnosis reduces their entire being and personality down to one word. No one can be summed up in one word or phrase. People who feel this way about a diagnosis may choose to describe their experiences, rather than tell other people the label assigned to them by the medical system.

The labels used in bullying and hate crime are very different. No one deserves to be insulted, or spoken about cruelly. It is disgusting behaviour to be cruel to someone because they are different. In fact, it is a criminal offence in the UK and many other countries around the world.

Some people experiencing disability and who have grown up having insults shouted at them sometimes try to take these insults and turn them into something new – something positive. This is referred to as reclaiming words. However, insults can only be reclaimed by people who have experienced those specific insults and want to take the power away from their attacker and their words. Using an insulting word to attack a person is not an act of reclaiming a word.

Frida Kahlo

(1907–1954)

Colours. That is definitely the first impression of Frida Kahlo. She is surrounded by colour. Her bed covers, the wall hangings and the box of paints she is using right now, contain all of the colours you can possibly imagine.

This is the first time Frida has decided to paint a picture of herself. Isn't that exciting? She isn't sure exactly what she is doing, but her instincts tell her how to dip the paintbrush in water, and mix the paints to create the right hue. Then she presses the tip of the brush against her sketchbook. She makes a mark, and then another, and then another. Since her accident, she has had to wear a **full-body cast**. Sometimes, she feels a little like her body belongs to the doctors who treat it and not to her. So, doing a painting of herself, the way she sees herself – bright colours blazing – is a way to take back a sense of control over her body and how others see it.

When Frida's father noticed her passion for painting, he built her an easel that was shaped to allow her to paint in bed more freely. This meant that Frida could paint on canvas as well as in sketchbooks.

Frida was a teenager when the accident happened. A bus she was riding with her boyfriend crashed, and she broke bones all over her body, including her back. These injuries added to the long-term effects she experienced as a result of having Polio as a child. After the accident, as well as having to wear a full-body cast, Frida had to stay in bed for months on end. It was during this period that she started taking her painting seriously. At first she painted and drew in her journal, but she soon began to make full-scale artworks as well.

Frida's style was unique. She often

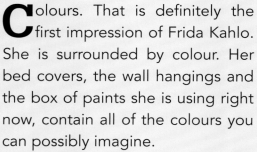

painted brightly coloured self-portraits that included references to nature, pain and folklore. In these she was fiercely honest, often painting in what others would see as flaws in her appearance. By including them, she challenged the ways other people saw her. She was also proud of her Mexican and indigenous **heritage**, and honoured it in her work.

Eventually Frida's body knitted itself back together and she learnt to walk again. However, she continued to experience chronic pain and disability throughout her life.

Frida was also a political activist. She was a **communist** and a feminist. She was also **bisexual** and campaigned for gay rights. There have been many books written about her and even films made about her life. Her paintings are featured in galleries all around the world to this day.

EXPLORE MORE:
Frida loved to express herself. Have you ever used art to express yourself?

WORDS TO KNOW
Bisexual: a person who falls in love with people who aren't only from one gender.
Communist: someone who believes that property should have shared ownership – with items owned as a community, rather than by individuals.
Full-body cast: made of plaster and covers most of a person's body. The cast helps to heal people's bones.
Heritage: the history, stories and culture that are passed from generation to generation among groups of people.

Frida Kahlo experienced **injuries from a bus crash**. She had multiple broken bones, and had displaced three of the small bones that made up her spine. She experienced chronic pain for the rest of her life as a result. Alongside these injuries, Frida experienced the long-term effects of having Polio as a child. This also affected her movement and the amount of pain she was in.

"FOR A FRIEND WITH AN UNDERSTANDING HEART IS WORTH NO LESS THAN A BROTHER."

Homer

(approx. 750 BCE)

In ancient Greece, we find Homer wandering the streets, carefully holding on to their **lyre**. They are looking for one house in particular where they are due to perform tonight. Homer isn't nervous; they do this nearly every night. They write epic poems about the world around them and then sing them, often to complete strangers, whilst strumming their lyre.

When Homer finally finds the house they are due to perform at, the hosts let them in and immediately offer them a drink and something to eat. The music will begin after dinner. Homer accepts the drink and food, and digs into a hunk of bread spread with honey. When the time is right, they take out their lyre and perform.

Homer was a poet who lived in the time of the ancient Greeks. No one knows if they were a man, woman or non-binary person. Although we know very little about Homer, many historians believe that they were Blind. Looking at Homer's life in ancient times shows us that disability has always existed.

Homer is the author of two well-known **epic poems**: *The Iliad* and *The Odyssey*. These tell the stories of Greek heroes around the time of the **Trojan War**. The poems are nearly 3,000 years old and are still taught in schools all around the world today.

Homer often used repeated vivid descriptions of the world they experienced. For example, using the phrase "rosy-fingered dawn" to help people imagine a sunrise, whether they could see one in front of them or not. This is an example of how being Blind may have impacted Homer's work. This also helped them to keep an even rhythm in their poems, which is very useful when setting them to music. At first, Homer's poems existed only as performance pieces. It was only much later on that they were written down.

EXPLORE MORE:
Creating stories can be very freeing. Many people find inventing stories helps them to work through things that happen in their lives.

WORDS TO KNOW

Epic poem: a really long poem that tells a story.
Lyre: a stringed musical instrument, a bit like a guitar crossed with a harp.
Trojan War: a war between the Trojans and the ancient Greeks.

It is thought by a number of historians that Homer was **Blind**. This means that they were unable to see for at least some of their life. They performed their poems out loud instead of writing them down, however this wasn't unusual as it was common for poets to perform their pieces at the time.

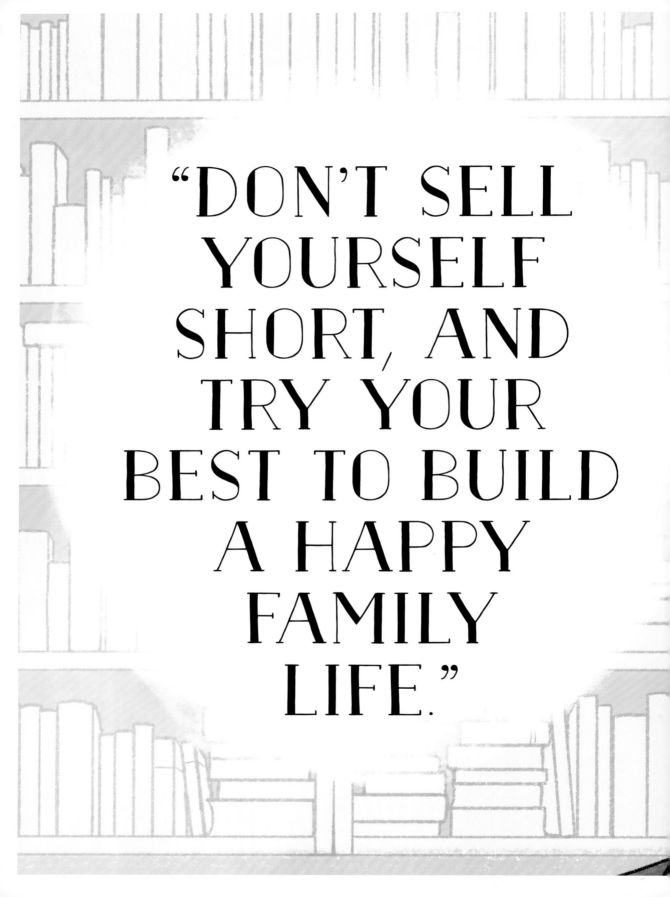

"DON'T SELL YOURSELF SHORT, AND TRY YOUR BEST TO BUILD A HAPPY FAMILY LIFE."

Zhang Haidi

(born 1955)

Zhang's mother is out of breath. She has Zhang's body slung over her shoulders. People are staring, but neither Zhang nor her mother care – this trip is important. They are going to school. As they approach the school gates, Zhang's mother puts Zhang down for a moment to catch her breath. She manages to pick her up again after a couple of minutes. They enter the school, determined to get Zhang an education.

They enter the headteacher's office and Zhang's mother helps her into a chair. Zhang's mother is prepared to carry Zhang to school every day, she is very keen for her daughter to get an education. Despite this, the headteacher says no. He states that the school does not permit people experiencing disability to enrol. When Zhang hears this she feels crushed. All she wanted to do was to learn, along with other children her own age.

As a young girl, Zhang very much wanted to go to school, so her mother carried her there on her back. When they arrived, the school refused to allow Zhang to take classes, purely because she had a

disability. People thought she was different to other children because she couldn't move her lower body.

Zhang didn't let the school's rules stop her. She taught herself lessons from books, all the way up to university level. She also learnt to speak four languages and later found work as a **translator**. As well as translating other people's writing, she has written several books herself.

Since the 1980s, Zhang has campaigned for disabled people's rights and makes **political** speeches. She wants to make sure that in the future, all children can go to school. Every body is different and nobody should be left out because of the way their body works.

EXPLORE MORE:

Why do you think it is important that all children get to go to school?

WORDS TO KNOW

Political: relating to the government, and how a country is run.
Translator: someone who knows at least two languages and uses their knowledge of two languages to change a piece of writing, or someone speaking, from one language to another.

Zhang Haidi experiences **Paraplegia**. This means that she cannot move her lower body and uses a wheelchair to get around.

"LOSING MY
HEARING HAS
MADE ME A
BETTER LISTENER
AND MUSICIAN
– SO MUCH SO
THAT IT HAS
TAKEN ME
ALL OVER THE
WORLD."

Evelyn Glennie

(born 1965)

Evelyn can no longer hear using her ears, but she is determined to be a musician. She has studied music for as long as she can remember, but now she can't hear her favourite pieces, or what she is playing. One day, Evelyn's music teacher takes her to one side. He holds her hand up against a drum. Evelyn doesn't understand what he is doing until he bangs the drum. Instantly, Evelyn feels the vibrations on the skin of the drum. Evelyn takes the drumstick from her teacher and hits the drum herself. She does this several times, and feels the difference in the vibrations depending on how hard she hits the drum. This is the start of Evelyn learning to hear with her body.

Evelyn Glennie was brought up to love music. Her parents adored it and they passed that passion on to their child. So, when Evelyn began to lose the hearing in her ears at the age of eight, everyone was worried.

When Evelyn was twelve years old, a doctor told her that she was officially deaf and would have to give up music. Evelyn and her parents disagreed. They thought that it wasn't up to the doctor to decide what Evelyn did with her life. So, Evelyn continued her piano lessons and began to play **percussion** instruments too.

As she lost the hearing in her ears, Evelyn learnt that listening is actually all about touch. She used her whole body to feel the vibrations of the music. This meant she could use her body as a gigantic ear. Using her body, she found that she could actually pick up smaller sounds than people who use their ears.

For example, the tiniest tinkle of a triangle played in a piece of music.

Evelyn now performs in huge **orchestras** and has released many solo albums. She led the drummers at the opening ceremony of the 2012 Olympic Games in London. She often performs barefoot, in order to sense the music more clearly.

Evelyn's story shows that no one should make assumptions about what people can or can't do.

- -

EXPLORE MORE:
Why do you think Evelyn's parents didn't listen to her doctor when he said she had to give up music?

- -

WORDS TO KNOW
Orchestra: a large group of people playing musical instruments.
Percussionist: a musician who plays the drums, cymbals, xylophone or another kind of instrument. They often keep the beat in a piece of music, but some songs are made up entirely of percussion instruments.

Evelyn Glennie is **deaf**. This means that she cannot hear using her ears. However, Evelyn can hear using the rest of her body.

EVERYTHING IS MADE OF STORIES

THINK OF A HAPPY EVENT THAT HAPPENED TO YOU AND YOUR FRIENDS.

GOT IT?

If you and your friends were to each, individually, describe that event, would you all tell the same story? Probably not. You would all focus on different things. Say it was a day on the beach – you might mostly tell the story of how you got that delicious chocolate ice cream. Meanwhile, one of your friends might focus on the story of the jellyfish that you all saw washed up on the sand. Another friend might tell the story of the water fight you had in the sea. You all experienced the same event, but you each came away with a different story. How you tell the story of the events in your life is part of what defines who you are.

People experiencing disability are told a lot of stories about themselves. The tellers of these stories – family, friends, doctors and teachers – often don't experience the disability themselves. The stories that other people tell about our experiences don't matter. The only thing that matters is the way that we see and express our own stories, and what we make of our own experiences.

You might find that writing things down, or drawing, is a good way to make sense of the story of your life. Tell it how you want. Your opinion is the only one that truly matters when it comes to your own story.

"TO REALIZE THERE'S LITTLE THINGS TO BE GRATEFUL FOR KEEPS YOU GOING."

Ellie Simmonds

(born 1994)

It just feels right. This is the first time Ellie has been in a swimming pool. She is getting lessons on how to swim, but she can barely focus on what the swimming teacher is saying. Instead, she focuses on the feel of the water on her skin. It is refreshing and smooth. She senses that if she let her body go she could float on the surface. She tries it out and quickly discovers that floating feels like flying. She starts paying attention to what the teacher is saying and begins to swim. Swimming feels like swooping through air. At the end of the lesson, she eagerly asks her parents how soon she can get back into the pool.

Ellie Simmonds has won many medals for her swimming. She joined the British **Paralympic** team at just thirteen years old. She was born with Achondroplasia and competes in the S6 swimming category. This means that Ellie competes with other swimmers experiencing similar conditions to hers. As well as winning medals for her swimming, Ellie has been awarded both an **MBE** and an **OBE** by Queen Elizabeth II for her services to sports.

Despite being such a strong swimmer, for a long time Ellie had a fear of swimming in the sea. She was afraid of the unknown – of what sea creatures might be lurking beneath her. She conquered

this fear by going on a trip to swim with dolphins.

Throughout her career, Ellie has used her fame to talk about disability in public. She has shown that people experiencing disability can be very capable at competing in sports.

EXPLORE MORE:
If you were competing in a sports contest, what event would you do?

WORDS TO KNOW
MBE and OBE: honours awarded by the Queen of the United Kingdom and the Commonwealth. They are given to people who have done amazing things.
Paralympics: every four years, thousands of disabled sportspeople compete in the Paralympics. It is an international sports competition.

Ellie Simmonds experiences **Achondroplasia**. This means that her arms and legs are shorter than they might have otherwise been.

"I LOVED MYSELF. AND WITH THAT, OPPORTUNITIES START TO FALL INTO MY LAP."

Winnie Harlow

(born 1994)

Winnie is not suffering. In her hand right now, is a newspaper that says otherwise. The **article** claims that Winnie is a model who "suffers" from Vitiligo. It is true that Winnie has a skin condition, but it is definitely not true that she is suffering from anything. Winnie rightfully feels a lot of irritation at the article, but she takes a deep breath and thinks hard about what to do next. She wants the newspaper to acknowledge that what it has said is wrong – that the article doesn't represent who she is. She decides to contact her lawyer and take legal action so that the newspaper has to correct how it described her.

Before Winnie Harlow went to school, she didn't see herself as different to anyone else. It was only when other pupils tried to make Winnie feel like she wasn't beautiful that she began to question herself.

The bullies thought that Winnie was different because of her skin condition. However, Winnie found that the best way to fight back against the bullies was to be confident as herself, and make sure that they knew that Vitiligo didn't make her any different to them.

Winnie became a **supermodel** when she was twenty years old,

and continues the fight she began at school by speaking up and trying to make a world where all women and girls can be seen as beautiful.

Winnie doesn't like to be described as "brave" as that suggests that there is something wrong with her looks, and that she has to be "brave" to go out and show herself to the world. There is nothing wrong with the way Winnie looks. Winnie prefers to describe herself as "confident". When a newspaper article suggested that Winnie was "suffering" from Vitiligo she called them out on it. She knows she is not "suffering" from anything – she is experiencing life with its ups and downs, as we all do.

The way we use language is very important, and the word "suffering" is one that many people experiencing disability find inaccurate and unhelpful.

- - - - - - - - - - - - - - -
EXPLORE MORE:
Why do you think that Winnie didn't want to be described as "suffering"? Do you think that people should be able to decide for themselves how their own condition is described?
- - - - - - - - - - - - - - -

WORDS TO KNOW
Article: a piece of writing included with others in a newspaper, magazine, or other publication.
Supermodel: a successful fashion model who has a global reputation and is famous.

Winnie Harlow experiences **Vitiligo**. This means that pale patches form on her skin.

"IT'S
PERHAPS
MORE COMMON
NOW FOR PEOPLE
TO SEEK OUT
PROFESSIONAL
HELP AND THAT'S
A GREAT
THING."

Kay
Redfield Jamison

(born 1946)

Kay's brain is going fast. Too fast. So fast, music seems to be running super slowly. So fast, she can't stop writing. She goes into the student bookshop and buys a huge pile of books. To her they all seem to be connected to her research, but to other people they look like a random selection. She places the teetering pile on her desk and it almost spills over. She dives into the books immediately, underlining paragraph after paragraph of text that might be useful to her research.

It's a month later. Kay's brain is going slowly – the opposite of how it was just last month. She can barely move. She doesn't want to get out of bed. The cocoon she's created out of a duvet and pillows is so safe and comfortable. Kay hasn't washed for a long time, but taking a shower seems like an impossibly complicated task to her right now. Even eating is difficult. She looks at the heaps of books on her desk and can't understand why she bought them in the first place.

When Kay was at university taking the courses that would lead to her training to be a doctor, she became very unwell. She was full of too much energy, which felt good at first, but then led to her ending up in dangerous situations. She didn't yet realize that she was experiencing Bipolar Disorder. Bipolar Disorder is a **mental health** condition, which affects people's mood.

Due to her experience of mood swings, Kay decided to study Psychology instead of Medicine.

Once she completed her course, she began to work for the university. This was when she finally looked for help from a **psychiatrist**. The psychiatrist diagnosed Kay with Bipolar Disorder.

After finding help from a psychiatrist, Kay decided that she wanted to use her skills as a **psychologist** to help people experiencing similar conditions to her. She knows that the treatment of mental health conditions and physical health conditions should be equally good. In her work as a psychologist, she makes sure that her patients get the high quality of care they deserve.

Kay is also the author of many books, including *Touched With Fire*, which is about how people with Bipolar Disorder are often very creative.

WORDS TO KNOW

Mental health: all about feelings and emotions. People with a mental health condition may have extreme emotions, or not feel much at all. They may also have unusual experiences, such as seeing things that other people can't see.

Psychiatrist: a type of doctor who looks after people experiencing mental health conditions.

Psychologist: a professional who understands how the mind works, and helps people experiencing mental health conditions.

Kay Redfield Jamison experiences **Bipolar Disorder**. This means that she experiences extreme moods that can be high or low. She also experiences times in between these mood swings, when her mood is less extreme. High mood is often called mania, low mood is often called depression.

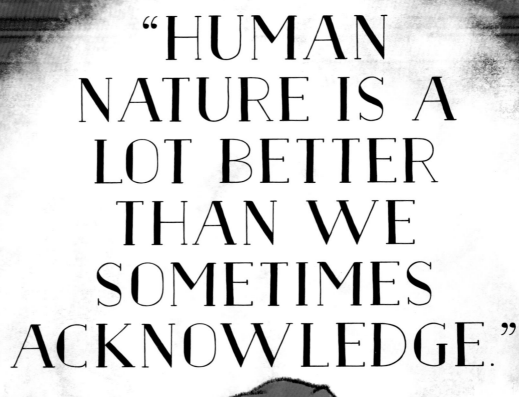

"HUMAN NATURE IS A LOT BETTER THAN WE SOMETIMES ACKNOWLEDGE."

David Blunkett

(born 1947)

David feels like he is always studying. He is taking evening classes, but even when he is at work during the day, he is going through his lessons in his head. As a child he didn't have much of an opportunity to study, so when he made the decision to go to university, he knew that he would first have to take evening classes to finish high school. He has been doing that for several years now. Working during the day, taking classes by night. He barely sleeps just to keep on top of it all. Still, nothing can squash his dream of going to university. He has a mission; he is going to become a politician.

David Blunkett was the first Blind **Cabinet Minister** in the UK. He had to work hard to become a politician; taking six years of evening classes to pass the exams he needed to get into university. During his time as a member of the Labour Party, he led a massive expansion in education, so that more people could go to university. He also started up the **Disability Rights Commission** and served as **Home Secretary**.

Lisa Bufano

(1972–2013)

The movements are slow at first. There is music playing, but it begins with a low drone to match the gradual movements. We see four Victorian table legs attached to the body of a woman. They move in carefully coordinated steps and missteps. They mimic the graceful movements of a doe approaching something she is curious about. The whole performance is packed with emotion. The dancer controlling the table legs is Lisa Bufano. She begins to match the shapes the legs are making with her entire body. She dances. It is beautiful. It is deeply moving; like her body has been holding some kind of tragic drama within itself and is now releasing it through dance.

After Lisa Bufano had her lower legs and fingers amputated at 21, she used her skills as a gymnast to create her very own style of dancing. She was a very inventive woman who used her body to **communicate** her emotions. She used art to show people who she really was, rather than them judging her based on her disability alone.

Her most famous dance involved attaching Victorian table legs to each of her limbs. She would then use her gymnastic skills to balance and move on them. Lisa also did a performance underwater, wearing a fin like a fish's tail. She described the way she could swap between different **prosthetic** limbs for different purposes, as being like having many bodies. She used many of her different bodies in her art. Lisa also made artworks in a variety of other forms, including painting and making sculptures.

EXPLORE MORE:

Dancing, like writing, is a way of creating stories — only these stories are told through your body. You can also create dances in your imagination.

WORDS TO KNOW

Communicate: to share information with someone — this can be through speaking, writing, sign language, or many other forms.

Prosthetic: an item that can be attached to the body to help it work the way the person using the prosthetic wants their body to work. For example, someone who has one leg may wear a prosthetic in order to walk.

Lisa Bufano experienced **multiple limb amputation** due to a bacterial infection. This means that her fingers and both of her legs below the knee had to be surgically removed in order to save her life. Lisa used a variety of prosthetic limbs to both get around, and to be creative in her performances.

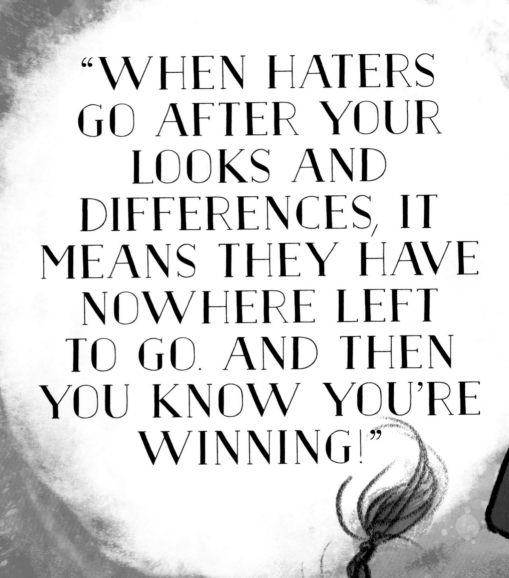

"WHEN HATERS GO AFTER YOUR LOOKS AND DIFFERENCES, IT MEANS THEY HAVE NOWHERE LEFT TO GO. AND THEN YOU KNOW YOU'RE WINNING!"

Greta Thunberg

(born 2003)

It's a Friday during term time, but Greta isn't at school. Instead, she is sitting on the steps that lead up to the Swedish Parliament building. Even though her arms are aching, she continues to hold her placard high up in the air. The sign reads "School Strike for the **Climate**".

For several months, Greta has been feeling depressed and has had difficulty eating and talking. It all started when she first learnt about **climate change** and how little is being done to stop it. She organized this protest as a way of releasing the feelings she has kept bottled up for so long.

In this moment, Greta is the only child on strike. Soon, that will change. Over the next few years, Greta will become the founder of a global movement. Millions of schoolchildren – all inspired by her stand against climate change – will gather to protest every Friday.

Greta Thunberg knows there is something wrong with the world: climate change – the negative effect we, as humans, are having on the planet. Greta knows that we should all be talking about it and trying to tackle it. So, she uses her voice to tell as many people as possible. She speaks in front of huge crowds about how we can save the planet if we all try really hard, right now. Greta also talks about climate change on television, and she has written a book about it with the help of her family.

Greta has a strong sense of justice. The way that she thinks – seeing things as clear-cut right or wrong – allows her to identify what needs to be done to fight against climate change. Although she is still a child, Greta is not afraid of standing up for what she believes in and making sure she is heard.

- -

EXPLORE MORE:

Do you know about climate change? It is one of the most urgent crises facing the human race. If you haven't been taught about it, it is worth doing some research into it.

- -

WORDS TO KNOW

Climate: the average measurements of temperature, wind, humidity, snow and rain in a place over the course of years. Climate is like the weather, but over a long time.

Climate change: a change in our planet's climate and weather patterns. At the moment, we are on the brink of a huge shift in Earth's climate due to global warming. Global warming is caused by the way humans currently live, especially the amount of fossil fuels we burn.

Greta Thunberg is **Autistic**, and she also experiences **Obsessive Compulsive Disorder (OCD)** and **Selective Mutism**. Experiencing these three conditions means that the way she thinks, reacts to the world and communicates with other people is different to many other people without her conditions. Greta's way of thinking means that she can clearly see that we must do something about climate change immediately.

"WHEN I FOUND I HAD CROSSED THAT LINE, I LOOKED AT MY HANDS TO SEE IF I WAS THE SAME PERSON."

Harriet Tubman

(1822–1913)

The air is thick with tension. This is the most risky part of the journey. They are approaching the Canadian border. Other people would have crumbled under the pressure, but Harriet is carefully controlling her feelings. She has made this journey many times before, but it isn't something anyone could get fully used to. The other people in the party will hopefully only need to make this trip once. The journey to freedom. The journey away from a life of slavery in the USA. Harriet is part of an organization known as the **Underground Railroad**. She helps people escape slavery, just as once someone helped her to escape.

Harriet Tubman was an activist who fought for the rights of Black people, women and people experiencing disability. She worked as a spy during the **American Civil War**. She was deeply religious and experienced visions that she believed were sent from God, which some experts now think was a result of her experiencing Epilepsy. She was also born into slavery, and it is thought that she developed Epilepsy after a slave owner struck her in the head while she defended another slave.

Harriet managed to escape from where she was being held

as a slave, and was helped by the Underground Railroad to complete her journey. Later on, she was brave enough to join the Underground Railroad herself and went back to the terrible place where she had been held, in order to rescue other Black people who were enslaved. To do this, she risked her life many, many times, and historians think she rescued hundreds of people.

EXPLORE MORE:
Harriet dreamt of a world where all human beings were free. She used her dreams to make the world a better place. What are your dreams for the future?

WORDS TO KNOW
American Civil War: a war fought in the United States of America between 1861 and 1865.
Civil war: a war that takes place when two or more groups within one country fight, rather than a war between two separate countries.
Underground Railroad: a secret network of free and enslaved Black people and white abolitionists in the 1800s made up of routes and safe houses, used to help slaves escape to places that had banned slavery, for example, Canada.

Harriet Tubman experienced **Epilepsy**. This means that she experienced seizures, extremely painful headaches and could abruptly lose consciousness. The visions she experienced may also have been part of her experience of Epilepsy.

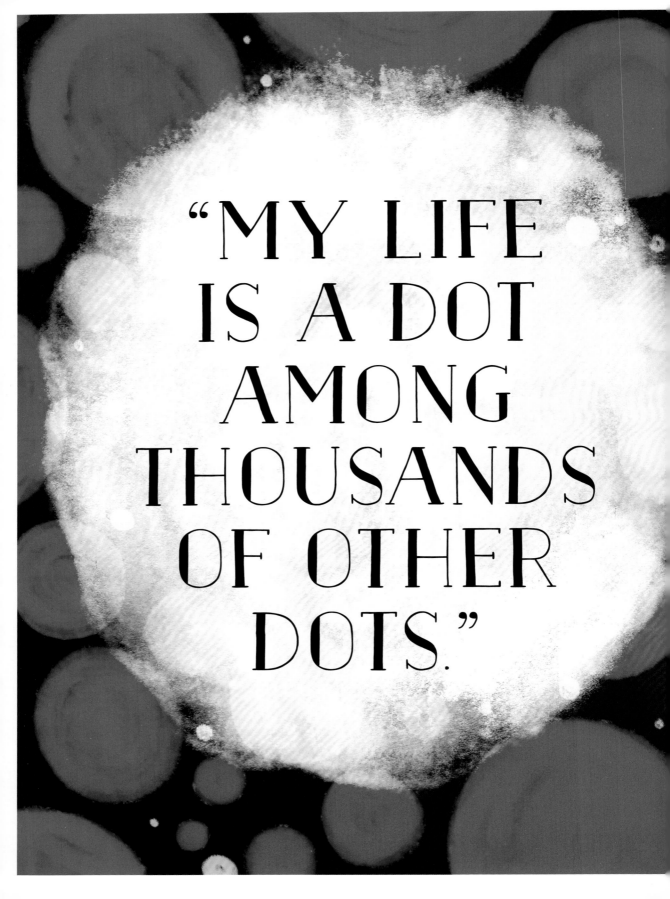

"MY LIFE IS A DOT AMONG THOUSANDS OF OTHER DOTS."

Yayoi Kusama

(born 1929)

One morning, when things were difficult at home, Yayoi wandered off. She found herself in a field of violets. She watched as the plants blew in the wind. Their purple heads formed an intricate pattern of dots. This pattern shifted with each breeze. Then it happened. The flowers began to speak to Yayoi, just like the flowers in *Alice's Adventures in Wonderland*. Yayoi ran home and hid in a cupboard.

Whilst her breathing was still ragged with panic, Yayoi took out her sketchbook. She carried a sketchbook and pencils everywhere. She began to draw the flowers that had been talking to her. As she drew, she started to regain control over her breathing and her heart stopped beating as quickly as it had been a few moments ago.

The talking flowers were Yayoi Kusama's first **hallucination**. As she grew older, she also heard animals speak to her. She would frequently see colourful dots dance in front of her eyes. Drawing became Yayoi's way of processing her hallucinations. She drew flowers, animals and patterns made up of dots. Drawing helped Yayoi feel in control, and she loved making pictures.

When Yayoi was a teenager, she wrote to the famous American artist, Georgia O'Keeffe. Of course, Georgia O'Keeffe's flowers often represented something quite different. Yayoi wrote to Georgia for advice – she wanted to pursue a career in art, but she wasn't sure how to go about it. She also sent Georgia some examples of her paintings. To Yayoi's surprise, Georgia wrote back, and praised Yayoi's artwork. When she received the letter, Yayoi made a decision. She decided to move to New York, where there were many other artists.

When she got to New York, Yayoi fought to have her work exhibited. However, she encountered a lot of racism and sexism from other artists. Some of the other artists even stole her ideas for pieces of art. Still, Yayoi eventually became a famous artist.

Today, Yayoi lives in Japan. She sleeps in a **psychiatric hospital** and spends all day in the building opposite, where she has established her art studio. She still makes art every day.

EXPLORE MORE:

Why do you think it is important to Yayoi to keep working on her art, whilst she stays in the hospital?

WORDS TO KNOW

Hallucination: an incident where someone sees, hears, touches, feels or smells something that other people can't see, hear, touch, feel or smell.

Psychiatric hospital: a type of hospital that specializes in treating people experiencing mental health conditions.

Yayoi Kusama experiences **Obsessive Compulsive Disorder (OCD)**. This means that she experiences obsessions about certain subjects and compulsions to carry out repetitive acts. These repetitive acts can be seen in the repeated shapes in many of her paintings. Yayoi also experiences hallucinations as a result of her condition. Her hallucinations also influence her artwork.

DISABLED ACTORS SHOULD PLAY DISABLED CHARACTERS!

O ver the past decade, an increasing number of films about people experiencing disability have been made. On the surface, this can be seen as progress but, despite the existence of many talented actors experiencing disability, filmmakers go to extreme lengths to cast non-disabled actors instead. They use make-up and even CGI to make these non-disabled actors look as if they experience a disability, rather than casting a person experiencing disability in the first place. The non-disabled actors who play disabled roles very often go on to win the top awards in the acting industry. All of this means that people experiencing disability have very little say in how we are portrayed on screen.

Some people argue that actors should be able to play any role and that it is all part of acting. Yet, if that was true, why aren't people experiencing disability cast as non-disabled people, just as easily as the reverse? After all, it takes the same amount of make-up and CGI to make a person experiencing disability appear to be non-disabled, as it does to make an non-disabled person appear to be experiencing disability.

"IT'S ABOUT THE LIFE YOU HAVE, NOT THE ONE YOU DON'T."

Adam Pearson

(born 1985)

Eyes. Have you ever taken some time to really consider eyes? Other people's eyes. Adam has always felt the awkward energy that comes from them. He has been the target of stares his entire life. He is walking down the street and he can feel people's stares bouncing off him. He keeps walking. He phones a friend and talks to them about a film they both saw last week at the cinema.

People still stare, but Adam concentrates on the discussion of the film. Film is one of his big interests, after all, he is an actor. Being an actor is often about being looked at. People watching your every move on a screen or a stage. When Adam became an actor, this part of the job was nothing new to him. He now frequently gets noticed on the street for his starring role in *Under the Skin*, or for his work on television.

Adam Pearson experiences Neurofibromatosis and since becoming an actor, he has spoken out about the lifelong bullying and harassment that occurs in his daily life just because people label him as being "different". For example, it is wrong and disrespectful to stare at anyone in public.

Adam's career took off when he acted in a film with movie star, Scarlett Johansson. The film was called *Under the Skin*. In it, Scarlett plays an alien being who has no idea what to expect from the life forms on Earth until she arrives here. She cannot see the "difference" in Adam's character's appearance that other humans label him with. This shows how the label of "different" is entirely invented by humans. A being with an outside point of view would be unable to see what many people see as being "different".

This message about difference is also vital to Adam's own activism. He brings attention to the bullying and **hate crimes** people experiencing Neurofibromatosis and other similar conditions live with. He also campaigns about the lack of opportunities for actors experiencing disability within the film industry.

- - - - - - - - - - - - - - - - - - - -

EXPLORE MORE:
Why do you think it is important to not bully people for the way they look?

- - - - - - - - - - - - - - - - - - - -

WORDS TO KNOW
Hate crime: when a crime is committed based on discrimination. For example, someone acting hostilely, insulting or attacking someone else, just because that person experiences a disability.

Adam Pearson experiences **Neurofibromatosis**. This means that his brain, spinal cord, nerves and skin can grow tumours, including on his face.

"DON'T ONLY PRACTISE YOUR ART, BUT FORCE YOUR WAY INTO ITS SECRETS."

Ludwig van Beethoven

(1770–1827)

Ludwig has invited two of his friends over. One of them is a philosopher, the other is a musician similar to Ludwig. Although they are alone in Ludwig's drawing room, they don't **communicate** by speaking. Instead, each of them scrawls what they want to say into a notebook, and then holds it out for the other two to see. Ludwig has a heap of these notebooks, already full of writing. He calls them his "conversation notebooks". The three men discuss life and the world, writing it all down. They do this because Ludwig is deaf, and **sign language** is not yet widely used or standardized. At the time, the notebooks were purely functional –

the easiest way for Ludwig to talk to his friends. However, as Ludwig grew to be a famous musician and composer, historians who are curious

about his thoughts on music and other issues now use the notebooks.

Ludwig was working as a pianist when he began to lose his hearing. However his experience of being deaf didn't end his career in music. Although he stopped performing, his career as a composer took off. The pieces of music he wrote are still famous today, almost two hundred years later. They are powerfully moving works of art.

Sign language wasn't widely used during Ludwig's lifetime, so he used 'conversation books' to communicate with other people via writing. These notebooks have preserved many of Ludwig's thoughts about music and **philosophy**, as well as personal conversations. They are an exciting record for his many generations of fans.

- -

EXPLORE MORE:

Ludwig invented a new career for himself when he became deaf. Why do you think that it is important for a person to be able to re-invent themselves and try new things throughout their lifespan?

- -

WORDS TO KNOW

Communication: this happens when two people send messages to each other in some form. These could be written, typed, spoken, signed, a symbol, or a facial expression.
Philosophy: the study of human thought, logic and knowledge.
Sign language: a system of communication using visual gestures and signs.

Ludwig van Beethoven was **deaf**. He lost his hearing in the middle of his musical career.

"I THINK IT'S IMPORTANT THAT THERE'S LOTS OF ROOM FOR THAT REAL SPONTANEOUS, CHAOTIC STUFF."

Jess Thom

(born 1980)

Jess is setting up a page on her website. She is nervous, but determined. She wants to use the **tics** she experiences, as part of Tourette's syndrome, to generate art. Part of this will involve working with musicians and academics to create a piece of **sound art**, and other pieces of **performance art**. However, she also wants to make something that the public can join in with. That is why she is setting up a webpage inviting anyone to make art based on recordings of her tics. In doing this, Jess transforms her Tourette's syndrome into a way of creating art. It becomes a superpower. She is "Touretteshero".

Jess's body makes movements and sounds without her permission. She will also say words that she didn't intend to say, for example "biscuit". This is part of the Tourette's syndrome that she experiences. "Touretteshero" is Jess's **alter ego**. She makes theatre with her involuntary movements and sounds included as part of the performance. By transforming into Touretteshero, Jess turns her condition into a superpower. Jess created this alter ego in order to celebrate the humour and creativity to be found within Tourette's syndrome. However, the roots of Jess's transformation didn't first come from making a show, but when she was watching one.

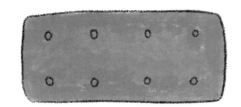

Jess was watching a live comedy show when it happened. Other members of the audience had complained about Jess's tics. Instead of standing up for Jess's right to watch the show with everyone else, the theatre staff took Jess to a soundproof booth to watch the rest of the show. This made Jess feel incredibly alone. At first she was too embarrassed by this experience to go back and see more shows, despite her love of comedy and theatre. Yet, with the support of her friends, Jess grew to change her perspective on things. She realised that if she was in control of the situation – by being the person performing – theatre could start to be part of her life again. As a result, Jess made a show called *Backstage in Biscuitland*, presenting the first public appearance of Touretteshero.

- -

EXPLORE MORE:
Why do you think having an alter ego can be useful?

- -

WORDS TO KNOW
Alter ego: a disguise that allows you to take on different traits for different situations. For example, Batman is the alter ego of Bruce Wayne.
Performance art: a piece of art which includes some form of live, or recorded performance.
Sound art: a form of art which involves making a piece of work out of different sounds.
Tic: a movement, sound, or spoken word made by a person's body without their intent.

Jess Thom experiences **Tourette's syndrome**. This means that her body makes movements and sounds without her permission.

"JUST GO OUT IN THE WORLD AND STRIVE TO BE WHAT YOU WANT TO BECOME."

Sudha Chandran

(born 1965)

Sudha takes a deep breath. She is in the wings (the space down the side of the stage she is about to perform on). She checks again that her costume is perfect. She uses a pocket mirror to check her make-up hasn't smudged. This performance needs to be amazing. It is all a lot of pressure. Sudha can hear her heartbeat thudding in her ears.

Outside, her friends and family have all gathered. Her best friend's laugh can be heard over the chattering. She knows that critics will be out there, too.

All too soon, it is time. Sudha takes to the stage and begins to dance. She enchants the entire audience. Sudha's dancing has always been something incredible. However, that is not the only reason why her friends and family are breathless at her immaculate performance. This is Sudha's first performance since she lost her right foot.

Sudha began dancing when she was three and a half years old. It was part of her daily life as a child – she went to school and then spent the evening dancing. However, she only fully realized how passionate she was about dancing when her entire dance career was in peril.

When Sudha was seventeen with many professional performances already behind her, she was in a major bus crash. Her injuries were minor – a fracture and some cuts.

However, the number of people in the crash meant that the hospital she was sent to was very busy. In amongst the hectic scene, the doctor treating Sudha forgot to wash one of her wounds before wrapping it in a bandage. As a result, Sudha's right foot became infected, and her parents made the decision to have it **amputated**.

After the amputation, Sudha's family and friends assumed she would never dance professionally again. They were wrong. Sudha was fitted with a **Jaipur leg**, which aided her recovery. It took three years, but Sudha learnt to dance again. She even mastered the complex moves of the **Bharatanatyam** style. Her first performance after her accident was sold out. Newspapers reported widely on it, and this led to Sudha receiving an offer to make a film about her life. She has since acted and danced in over one hundred films and TV series.

WORDS TO KNOW

Amputation: when someone's limb is removed. This is often done to prevent the spread of infection to the rest of the body.
Bharatanatyam: a form of Indian classical dance.
Jaipur leg: a form of prosthetic leg commonly used in India.

Sudha Chandran experiences having an **amputated foot**. Her foot was surgically removed as a result of an infection. Sudha wore a Jaipur leg in order to dance again after the amputation.

SOCIETY HAS IT WRONG!

The Social Model of Disability

The Social Model of Disability is used by disability activists and organizations to describe the way that society disables people, rather than an individual's health condition. This means that the pressure is on society to change, rather than individuals. People are often taught that the opposite is true – that if people experiencing disability want to survive, we have to try to adapt ourselves to behave the way society demands. This is wrong. Instead, everyone should all work together to remove the barriers to doing things that people experiencing disability encounter in society.

For example, Amy is a wheelchair user. She is very excited about the latest superhero film being released at the cinema. Her mum books tickets for the two of them to go. However, they have to go to a cinema they haven't been to before, as it was the only cinema showing the film at a time when they were free to go and see it. For the entire bus journey there, Amy tells her mum all about the other superhero movies in the series and her excitement is obvious. Finally, Amy and her mum arrive at the cinema.

Amy's heart drops when she sees the door. There is no ramp leading up to the door, and even if there had been, the doorframe is not wide enough for Amy's electric wheelchair to get through. It is clear that she will not even be able to get into the building. Amy is extremely disappointed.

In this scenario, Amy is disabled by the structure of society. When the cinema building was designed, the needs of people experiencing disability, including Amy's, weren't considered. Amy would be perfectly able to see the film at the cinema if her needs, and the needs of other wheelchair users, had been considered when the cinema was being built. Lots of buildings are inaccessible to people experiencing disability, including schools, workplaces and shops. This is an example of a physical barrier.

Let's rewind Amy's story to earlier that morning. Here we will find another example of how society disables people.

Amy and her mum rely on buses and trains to travel, so today, they are getting the bus to the cinema. They have looked it up and it should stop right outside. Amy and her mum head to their local bus stop and wait.

When the bus arrives, Amy gets ready to board it. Amy's mum asks the bus driver if Amy can use the ramp that he keeps next to his seat. The bus driver takes one look at Amy's wheelchair and refuses to let her get on the bus. He says that the bus only has one space for people experiencing disability and someone is already using it. As the bus speeds off, Amy spots that the space for a wheelchair isn't being used by another wheelchair user, but by someone who has two large suitcases. This is not an appropriate use of a space for people experiencing disability.

The bus driver and the passenger with the suitcases both actively disable Amy in this example. Their attitude regarding the appropriate use of the wheelchair space on the bus means that Amy is not able to get to the cinema on time. These attitudes about disability are a huge part of how society disables people. This is an example of an attitudinal barrier.

Society disabling people is far from applying only to people who use wheelchairs. Most of the people in this book will have encountered barriers in society.

Only some of these barriers are physical – including being able to get into, and move around buildings. Some people included in this book might have encountered an attitudinal barrier to them working, for example if they are told they have to work full-time, even though they get tired more easily than a non-disabled person. Others might need personal assistants to help them complete daily tasks, and so remove numerous barriers in the process.

One of the methods for removing societal barriers is called access support. Access support aims to even the playing field between people experiencing disability and non-disabled people, so that we can fairly pursue the same opportunities. Hiring a personal assistant, or adapting a building so that it is suitably accessible, costs money. This money is on top of the living costs that non-disabled people also have to cover, making living with disability more expensive than living without disability. For this reason it is important that there is a functioning welfare system, and other access funding from the government, to support the lives of people experiencing disability.

The Social Model of Disability is largely thought to be opposed to the Medical Model of Disability. The Medical Model puts a heavy emphasis on a person's diagnosed condition, and puts pressure on that person to change, instead of focusing on how society limits the opportunities for people with that diagnosis. However, some people experiencing disability may prefer to use the Medical Model to describe their symptoms, or a mixture of both the Social Model and the Medical Model.

- -

Al-Aman Organization for Blind Women's Care (AOBWC),
founded by Fatima Al-Aqel

"...AIMS AT FULFILLING TOTAL INVOLVEMENT OF BLIND WOMEN IN SOCIETY."

Fatima Al-Aqel

(1957–2012)

Fatima is here today to open her school. This project has been in her mind's eye for years. A dream at first, but now it is something more solid – an actual building. One filled with people who know what needs to be done, and who have the knowledge to follow through. In many ways, this is Fatima's moment. In other ways, it is the students' moment. All the prospective pupils who thought that their education was over when they began experiencing **sight loss**. Instead, they will now be educated here at Fatima's school. Getting an education will change their lives for ever.

In 1995, Fatima opened the first **Yemeni** school for women and girls experiencing sight loss. It was an intensely personal project. Fatima was studying at university when she lost her own sight. She had to fight to be allowed to finish her degree. When she did, she decided to use her knowledge about the world to help other Blind and partially sighted Yemeni women.

In the Yemen, where Fatima lived, the experiences of sight loss and being Blind were very common due to their lack of access to medical care. Education for women with these experiences was often cut short. In the same way that Fatima fought to complete her degree, she also fought for other women affected by sight loss to receive an education. She wanted all Yemeni women to be able to be part of society. Fatima found that this support was especially important for women living in rural areas, where access to healthcare, education and employment is even more sparse.

During her lifetime, Fatima also started a wider organization for Yemeni women and girls who are Blind, the Al-Aman Organization for Blind Women's Care.

EXPLORE MORE:
What is your favourite subject at school?

WORDS TO KNOW

Sight loss: when someone experiences a deterioration of their eyesight. Sometimes people will eventually go blind due to sight loss, sometimes they will lose only some of their vision.

Yemeni: refers to people who live in Yemen.

Fatima Al-Aqel was **Blind**. This means that she lost her sight whilst studying at university.

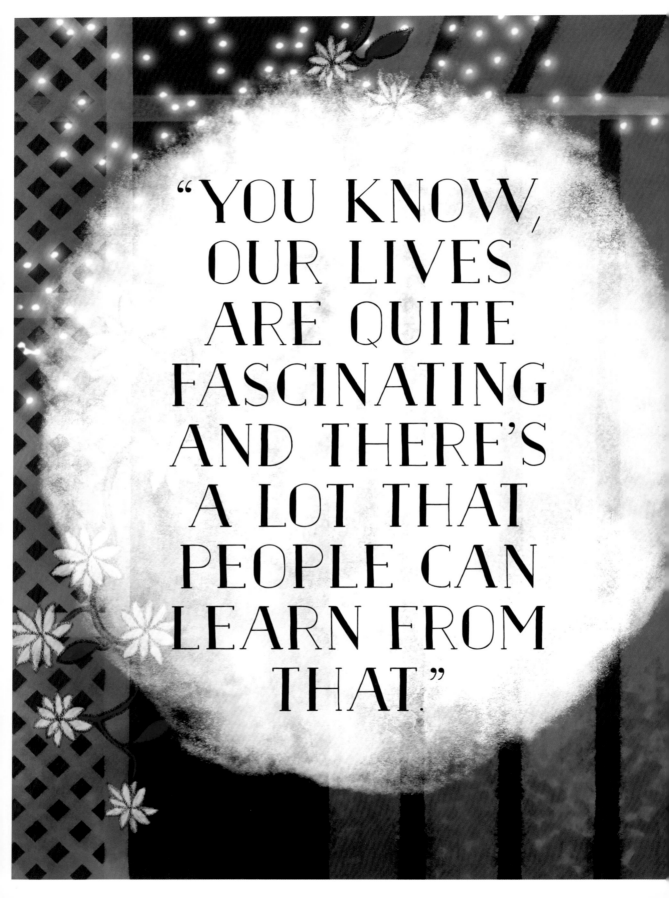

"YOU KNOW, OUR LIVES ARE QUITE FASCINATING AND THERE'S A LOT THAT PEOPLE CAN LEARN FROM THAT."

Liz Carr

(born 1972)

- - - - - - - - - - - - - - - - - -

Liz is in love and it's her wedding day. The ceremony is a busy one, packed with people from all walks of life, all there to celebrate with Liz and her soon-to-be wife, Jo. Although the ceremony is very important, the most exciting part of the wedding is still to come – the **wedding reception**. Liz and Jo have been practising their first dance for weeks. They have something very special in mind. They are going to do the main dance number from *Dirty Dancing*, one of their favourite films.

The dance involves Liz being lifted up into the air in her wheelchair, so they've drafted in the local fire brigade to hold her aloft at the exact right moment.

Liz started her performance career as a comedian. She used her act to explore themes of disability with her unique sense of humour, and also presented comedy radio shows.

Liz's career as an actor kicked off when she was cast as Clarissa Mullery in the popular BBC drama *Silent Witness*. Her character experiences the same condition as Liz: Arthrogryposis Multiplex Congenita. Liz took the sharp wit she relied on as a **comedian** and brought it to this role, defying the standard expectations usually assigned to actors experiencing disability.

Liz's comedy and acting breaks down barriers and discusses disability in new, very funny, ways.

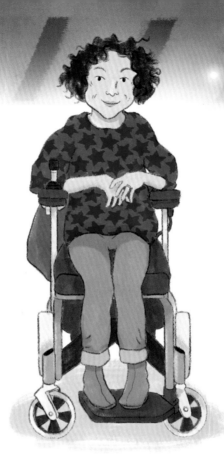

EXPLORE MORE:
Why do you think it is important that people experiencing disability have a place to express themselves using comedy?

WORDS TO KNOW
Comedian: someone whose performances, either on stage or on screen, are designed to make their audiences laugh.
Wedding reception: a meal and party held after a wedding.

Liz Carr experiences **Arthrogryposis Multiplex Congenita**. This means that her joints are shortened at multiple points in her body. As a result Liz uses an electric wheelchair.

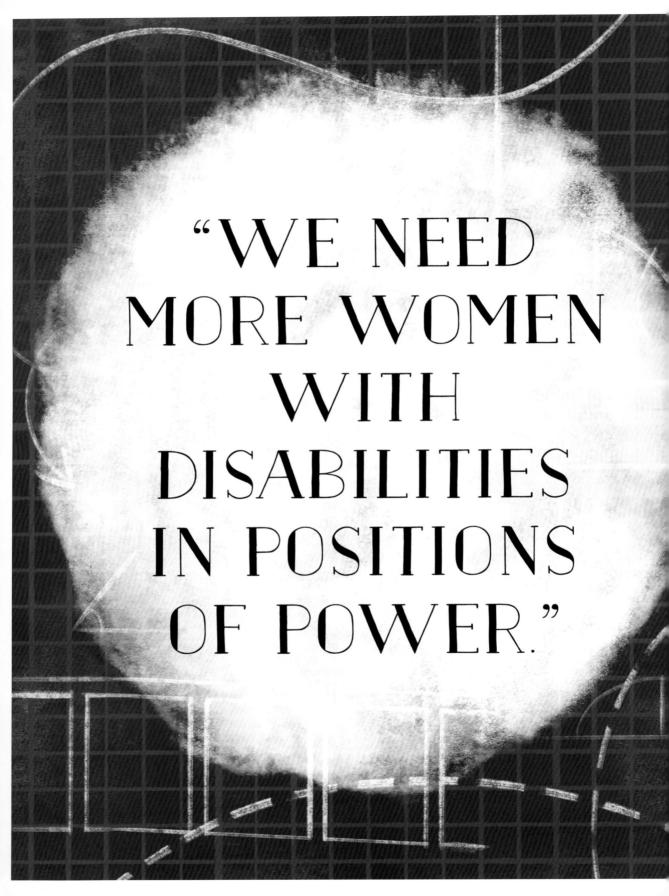

"WE NEED MORE WOMEN WITH DISABILITIES IN POSITIONS OF POWER."

Ola Abu Al Ghaib

(born around 1981)

O la is not studying architecture or engineering, yet she has spent a lot of her life at university discussing designs of buildings. She has been helping the university to make their campus more accessible to students experiencing disability. Right now she is having a meeting with three engineers, about how to install ramps and wider doorframes, so that wheelchair users can get inside all of their classrooms.

Ola can't walk or move her right hand. When she started university, the campus wasn't accessible at all, making it very difficult for Ola to get to her own classes. She campaigned for equal access and the university put her on the campus construction committee. In this role, she oversees adaptations to the campus to make it accessible to all students.

Being on the campus construction committee was only the start of Ola's life-long work as an advocate. After she completed her degree, helping to make university education more accessible along the way, she founded the Stars of Hope society. She also went on to do high-level research into disability access needs. She works to encourage

governments around the world to follow the **United Nations Convention on the Rights of People with Disabilities**. Her main focus is on countries in the Middle East, but she goes wherever she is needed.

Ola's biggest ambition is for people experiencing disability to be part of their community, no matter where they live, especially if their community is also **marginalized** in other ways.

- -

EXPLORE MORE:
What could be done to improve access at your school?

- -

WORDS TO KNOW

Marginalization: this happens when one group decides that another group is "different" or "other" to the way they think people should be, and therefore excludes them from society. People may be marginalized because of their race, religion, sexuality, gender or disability, among others. This has practical consequences, such as a lack of access to healthcare or human rights.

United Nations Convention on the Rights of People with Disabilities: a set of guidelines, agreed by many countries around the world, which focuses on the human rights of people experiencing disability.

Ola Abu Al Ghaib experiences **Paralysis due to a surgical accident**. This means that she cannot walk or move her right hand. As a result she uses a wheelchair.

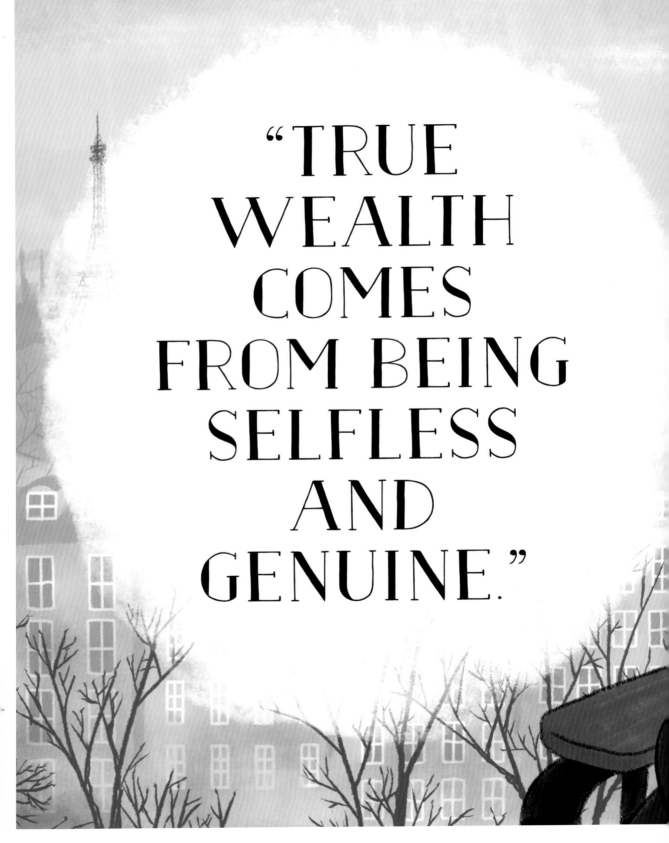

"TRUE WEALTH COMES FROM BEING SELFLESS AND GENUINE."

Jean Christophe Parisot

(born 1967)

Jean is on his way to work. Two **personal assistants** help him into the back of his van. There is a lift that goes up until his wheelchair is level with the entrance to the van, then the two personal assistants help him inside. They set off. It is quite a bumpy ride along the roads of Paris. On the way there, Jean gets a phone call. One of his personal assistants picks up the phone and holds it to his ear. It is a very important call, from someone at the heart of the French government. At the end of the call, Jean agrees to meet the politician in his office later in the afternoon. His personal assistant makes a note of this and searches for a space in Jean's hectic calendar. Once they arrive at the office, Jean is helped out of the van and through the doors to his workplace. All three people take a lift up to the right floor.

Jean works very long hours. Sixty hours a week. That's on top of the four hours of medical treatment he needs each day for his Tetraplegia. He is a **civil servant** who helps the French government make decisions. He is particularly involved in making sure that the rights of people experiencing disability are represented. In order to deepen his work on disability rights, he co-founded the Collective of Disabled Democrats in 2000.

As Jean finds it difficult to write, or

type, he uses his amazing memory to keep an impressive amount of information in his head. When Jean receives a phone call, he needs someone to hold the phone to his ear.

As well as improving the lives of people experiencing disability through his work, Jean is proof to society at large that people experiencing disability can achieve incredible things. He has even run for president, to prove that people experiencing disability can.

Jean has the support of his personal assistants, which enables him to keep working. This kind of support helps to level the playing field between people experiencing disability and non-disabled people. Tailored support can enable people experiencing disability to take on work on our own terms, and allows us access to our dream jobs. Too often, governments around the world try to strip away this support by refusing to fund it. Jean is one of many activists who work tirelessly to ensure that support is available to as many people experiencing disability as possible.

- -

EXPLORE MORE:

Experiencing disability can come with a lot of additional costs, such as personal assistants and adaptations to the home and workplace. Why do you think it is important that the government should help fund these costs?

- -

WORDS TO KNOW

Civil servant: someone who has a job advising the government.
Personal assistant: someone who works for a person experiencing disability, helping them with tasks when their employer (the person experiencing disability) requests it.

Jean Christophe Parisot experiences **Tetraplegia**. This means that he can't move his legs, arms or torso. He uses a wheelchair, which is moved around by personal assistants.

NOTHING ABOUT US, WITHOUT US!

"Nothing about us, without us" is a phrase commonly used by disability activists. It refers to the way that far too many decisions are made about people experiencing disability, by people who have no experience of disability themselves. For example, most groups that make decisions about the lives of people experiencing disability – governments, charities and individual organizations – don't employ enough, or, in some cases, any, people experiencing disability. Often people experiencing disability aren't even asked their opinion on pieces of work that will affect how we live. This is wrong. Every decision made about people experiencing disability should involve the contribution of those same people. This means that more governments, charities and organizations need to offer people experiencing disability jobs where their voices will be heard.

"DON'T LET ANYBODY PUT YOU DOWN BECAUSE OF YOUR DISABILITY."

Emmanuel Ofosu Yeboah

(born 1977)

Emmanuel is exhausted. He has been cycling for days. The effort of propelling himself forward becomes more difficult with each turn of the pedals on his bike. He pedals using one leg, as his other is shortened due to missing a shinbone. Emmanuel has a mission: to cycle the four hundred miles across the width of Ghana. He wants to raise awareness of how people experiencing disability are treated in his home country. To do this, Emmanuel needs media attention – and he pulls it off. Articles are written about his journey and he is interviewed by the international press. Eventually, books – and even a film – are made about him. All of this work puts disability and people experiencing disability's rights at the forefront of the public's minds.

After Emmanuel's mammoth cycle trek across Ghana, he won a prize from Nike for his work as a **triathlete**. He now uses a **prosthetic** limb. He used the award money to open schools, which equally value pupils

experiencing disability, and non-disabled pupils. This ambition came from his own past; as a child he had wanted to be educated among his non-disabled friends, but the system at the time made this very difficult. Emmanuel hopes that the schools he has set up will enable more Ghanaian children experiencing disability to go to school, and when they are there, not experience the bullying that Emmanuel himself endured as a child. He also wants to make sure that Ghanaian children experiencing disability don't have to pay extra for their schooling.

EXPLORE MORE:

If you wanted to bring attention to the human rights of people experiencing disability, or another cause that you are passionate about, what would you do?

WORDS TO KNOW

Prosthetic: a prosthetic is a man-made limb that can be used by people to help with their movement.
Triathlete: an endurance athlete who competes in triathlons. Therefore, a triathlon involves long distance cycling, swimming and running, all as part of one sports event.

Emmanuel Ofosu Yeboah experiences having **no shinbone in his right leg**. This means that his right leg couldn't function, and he had surgery to enable him to wear a prosthetic in order to walk.

"I AM GLAD THAT I HAVE HELPED PEOPLE. BUT I DON'T WANT TO STOP WORKING!"

Abraham Nemeth

(1918–2013)

- -

Abraham can't believe the words that are coming out of his teacher's mouth. She is telling him that he can't follow his dream to study to become a mathematician. Abraham is a star pupil, but it doesn't matter how well he does in his exams. His teacher is telling him that he can't study **mathematics**, not because of any lack of skill, but because he is Blind. At this point in history, **braille** is still being developed. There aren't yet any braille translations of mathematical symbols. How will Abraham read the mathematical texts for university, let alone write his essays?

At first, Abraham takes his teacher's remarks on board. As predicted, he does well in his school exams, but he studies two degrees in Psychology rather than his favourite subject. Later on, however, he changes tack. He becomes determined to find a way for Blind and partially sighted people to become mathematicians. This eventually leads to him creating a great invention; a braille system for mathematical symbols, called the Nemeth Braille Code for Mathematics and Science Notation.

As well as inventing the Nemeth Braille Code, Abraham invented a second method to help mathematicians affected by sight loss. This second invention was called MathSpeak. He first developed it for use in his own practice as a mathematician, so that he could easily write down his ideas, via recording his voice using a Dictaphone, and giving the recording to an assistant for them to transcribe into the final text. MathSpeak is a type of screen reader that correctly reads out mathematical symbols from written texts.

Using his inventions, Abraham finally studied mathematics to a very high level, and also taught at several universities. His work as a teacher and academic meant that he used his two inventions on a daily basis. His teacher should never have discouraged Abraham's mathematics career, but in the end he managed to get to the place he dreamt of as a teenager.

- - - - - - - - - - - - - - - - - - - -

EXPLORE MORE:
What would be your dream job? What do you need to do to get there?

- - - - - - - - - - - - - - - - - - - -

WORDS TO KNOW
Braille: a system of risen dots on a piece of paper, that make up words. This enables people who are Blind to read.
Mathematics: a form of study that involves numbers, and what they can tell us about the world.

Abraham Nemeth was **Blind**. This means that he couldn't see. He could read literature using braille, but he had to invent his own symbols in order to read mathematical texts.

RIGHTS NOT CHARITY

- -

"Rights, not charity" is another phrase commonly used by disabled activists. It refers to a rejection of a charity system that often makes decisions about people experiencing disability, without employing people who have those experiences in senior positions at their organization. Often charities don't even consult the disability community before making decisions. Although there are some disability-led charities, unfortunately they are rare.

Instead of the current charity system, activists experiencing disability campaign for us to have equal access to the human rights enjoyed by non-disabled people. This means that people experiencing disability should be offered opportunities and help with our higher cost of living as part of a fair, wide-ranging, and flexible system, led by our governments. This would enable people experiencing disability to not be dependent on charities, run by people who don't experience disability themselves; and allow people experiencing disability to make more decisions about how we live our own lives. This would be much more in line with our human rights. In order for this to work, governments need to employ people experiencing disability in positions where they can influence policy. An example of this in action is the United Nations Convention on the Rights of Persons with Disabilities. This convention pushes forward the human rights of people experiencing disability, rather than reliance on a charity system.

The phrase "rights not charity" also has a lot to do with rebelling against how people experiencing disability are seen by society. Disability activists campaign to not be seen as objects of pity, or the opposite – seen as "brave" people who deserve to be put on a pedestal just for existing while experiencing a disability. These two images are all too common in charity advertising and marketing materials. Neither of the two images represents true equality for people experiencing disability.

True equality can only come when people experiencing disability have access to the same rights, and esteem, as non-disabled people.

- -

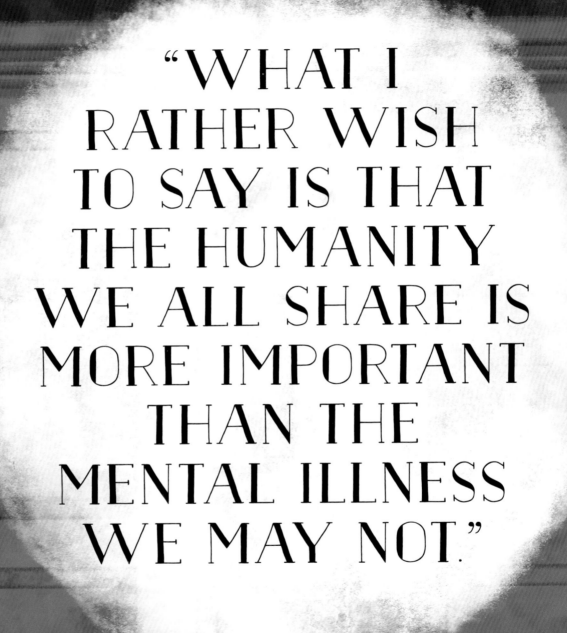

"WHAT I RATHER WISH TO SAY IS THAT THE HUMANITY WE ALL SHARE IS MORE IMPORTANT THAN THE MENTAL ILLNESS WE MAY NOT."

Elyn Saks

(born 1956)

Elyn is a lawyer – a job that involves a lot of talking. Usually, she is very eloquent, and people know exactly what she means, but for the last two weeks that hasn't been the case. Elyn's words have been coming out all mixed up, and her friends and colleagues don't know what she is trying to say. Elyn is scared. She hasn't opened her curtains for weeks, and she is finding it very difficult to remember to eat. She has also been having strange experiences; earlier that week, she turned around and saw a man holding a knife, but no one else around her could see the man. She also sometimes feels that she could set off explosions using her brain.

Elyn could have ended up spending her entire life in a hospital. When she was a young woman, she was diagnosed as having Chronic Schizophrenia. Schizophrenia is a condition that affects someone's perception of the world. People experiencing Schizophrenia might see, hear, taste, smell or touch things that other people can't. Their speech might be disorganized. They may also experience delusions – believing something is true, when no one else believes it so. Elyn was told that her situation was "grave". This meant that her doctors assumed that she would never be able to live and work independently. It took Elyn many years to get there, but she eventually proved her doctors wrong. She studied law at a top American university and eventually became a professor.

However, over the years, Elyn has ended up spending a lot of time in various hospitals. While she was in hospital, many of the staff described her as "schizophrenic". When they used this word to describe her, it made her feel like her **diagnosis** eclipsed her personality, and that she was some kind of walking diagnosis. Elyn does not agree with using the word "schizophrenic". For her, "schizophrenics" don't exist, only people living with Schizophrenia. This is an example of person-first language: language that puts the person before their diagnosis. Some people and groups of people experiencing disability prefer person-first language, while others prefer identity-first language, including many Blind, Deaf and Autistic people. Some people may prefer different language to these two types, or language unique to them.

Elyn was helped along her path with support from her friends, the right doctors, **psychoanalysts** and having a supportive workplace. She is an advocate for more people experiencing Schizophrenia getting this kind of support, rather than being stuck in the hospital system, ending up homeless or in prison. Elyn uses her knowledge of the law, as well as the insight gained from her own experiences, to promote people getting extensive support in the community. She also wants to change the way that employers consider employees – so that more workplaces don't just tolerate, but embrace people experiencing mental health conditions.

- - - - - - - - - - - - - - - - - - - -

EXPLORE MORE:

Why do you think it is important not to only define a person by their diagnosis, and to see them as someone who has had a wide variety of life experiences?

- - - - - - - - - - - - - - - - - - - -

WORDS TO KNOW

Diagnosis: a label that a doctor gives a person based on a pattern of symptoms.
Psychoanalyst: someone who talks to a patient and tries to help them understand the ways their brain works.

Elyn Saks experiences **Schizophrenia**. This means that there are periods in her life when she can't tell what is real, and what her mind has invented.

Judith's sister, Joyce:

"AND NOW I UNDERSTAND: OUR CONNECTION, HOW IMPORTANT IT WAS, HOW TOGETHER WE FELT EACH PIECE OF OUR WORLD, HOW SHE TASTED HER WORLD AND SEEMED TO BREATHE IN ITS COLOURS AND SHAPES."

Judith Scott

(1943–2005)

Judith moves her hands in a careful rhythm. Weaving, and pulling, and stitching brightly coloured wool. She is wrapping a set of objects – including a bicycle wheel propped up on top of a chair – creating a cocoon. Judith uses this method to make her startling artworks.

As Judith goes on making the piece, it slowly grows outwards with each wind of wool. This one piece will take her many months to complete. As she goes, she threads more objects into the piece – beads from her necklace, as well as rings and scarves that she had been wearing. She even takes other people's belongings and wraps them up with the rest of the objects.

Judith comes here – to the Creative Growth Art Studio – five days a week to work on her art. Whilst here, she gets completely absorbed in her work, always plotting what to make next. When she has finished a piece she makes a signal using her hands – sweeping them against each other. This lets one of the Creative Growth assistants know that she is ready to put her latest piece into storage. Once Judith has completed a work, they are

frequently exhibited in some of the top art galleries in the world.

Often Judith's artworks involve pairs of objects, wrapped up together, safe. This is possibly a symbol for Judith and her twin sister Joyce.

Judith discovered art late on. She had been unable to communicate using words throughout her entire life, so when she invented her own way of communicating, using **textile art**, an explosion of untold stories emerged in her intricate woven works. It was Judith's twin sister, Joyce, who first introduced Judith to art.

Judith and Joyce spent the first seven years of their life together. They were inseparable – joined together in a sensory world – able to communicate without speaking. As they did everything together, they were both devastated when they were split up. This happened when Judith's doctor recommended that she was sent to the Columbus State Institution, whilst her sister stayed at home. The doctor made this recommendation because Judith had been diagnosed with Down's syndrome.

Judith was supposed to go to school at the institution, but once she got there, it was decided that she would be unable to take part in school activities. This decision was based on a spoken test. Judith couldn't understand what was being said during the test because she

was Deaf. It took several decades for anyone to realize that Judith couldn't hear.

Thirty-five years after the twins were split up, Joyce fought to be reunited with her sister, and to get her out of the institution where she was being held. Joyce was eventually successful and the sisters lived close to each other until Judith's death.

Once they were back together, Joyce took Judith to the Creative Growth Arts Centre in Oakland, USA.

For the first two years Judith wasn't particularly interested in art. It wasn't until she watched a class on textile art that she picked up materials and began to make her work. Judith spent the last eighteen years of her life making art. She went to the art centre five days a week, apart from a short break when she had heart surgery. Judith is one of many **Outsider Artists** that the Creative Growth Centre has developed. Her work is now known all around the world.

EXPLORE MORE:
Why do you think it is important that everyone gets an education?

WORDS TO KNOW

Outsider Artist: someone who creates artwork outside of the system of galleries and art schools that make up the traditional art world.

Textile art: a method of creating artworks that include fabrics, wool, thread or other textiles.

Judith experienced **Down's syndrome** and being **Deaf**: this means that she had an extra chromosome in her cells (cells are the building blocks that make up a person).

FURTHER READING

- -

Scope

is a disability equality charity that covers England and Wales. Their community includes many people experiencing disability.

www.scope.org.uk/

Rethink Mental Illness

is an organization that supports people experiencing severe mental illness.

www.rethink.org/

Young Minds

is a charity which supports children and young people experiencing mental health conditions.

www.youngminds.org.uk/

The United Nations Convention on the Rights of People with Disabilities

is a convention that focuses on the human rights of people experiencing disability.

www.un.org/development/desa/disabilities/convention-on-the-rights-of-persons-with-disabilities.html

www.un.org/en/universal-declaration-human-rights/

www.youthforhumanrights.org/what-are-human-rights/universal-declaration-of-human-rights/articles-1-15.html

Young DaDaFest

is a yearly festival celebrating the artwork of young artists experiencing disability.

www.dadafest.co.uk/what-we-do/festivals-and-events/young-dadafest/

HELPLINES

ChildLine

ChildLine is a private and confidential service for children and young people up to the age of 19. You can contact a ChildLine counsellor about anything – no problem is too big or too small.

www.childline.org.uk/

Samaritans

If you are having a difficult time and you need someone to talk to, you can contact the Samaritans.

www.samaritans.org

Mental health:

If you are struggling with your mental health wellbeing or would like some tips, you can visit the NHS website.

www.nhs.uk/livewell/youth-mental-health/pages/Youth-mental-health-help.aspx

ABOUT
THE AUTHOR

Louise Page is a writer and artist who experiences complex mental illness. She lives at home with her parents, one moody cat and two adorable rabbits. When she isn't writing or making films and theatre, she can be found with her head buried in a book.

ABOUT
THE ILLUSTRATOR

Kat Williams is an illustrator whose favourite things to draw are people and animals. She also likes hiking, yoga and a strong cup of coffee. Kat lives in Leeds, where she shares a studio with another illustrator and a number of large, leafy houseplants.

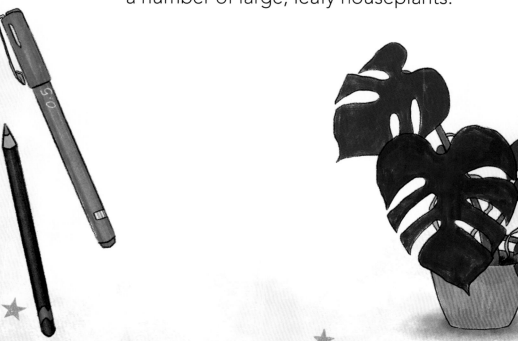

INDEX